C000170511

FRANCIS FRITH'S

A TASTE OF EAST ANGLIA

*In anticipation of some great meals, with
all my love, Julie xxx*

THE FRANCIS FRITH COLLECTION

www.francisfrith.com

FRANCIS FRITH'S

A Taste of
EAST ANGLIA

REGIONAL RECIPES FROM CAMBRIDGESHIRE,
ESSEX, NORFOLK AND SUFFOLK

Illustrated with historical photographs from
The Francis Frith Collection

FRANCIS FRITH'S

A Taste of
EAST ANGLIA

Ipswich, Buttermarket 1893 32204

Compiled by Julia Skinner

First published in the United Kingdom by
The Francis Frith Collection exclusively for Identity Books in 2009.
Paperback Edition ISBN 978-1-84589-454-2

British Library Cataloguing in Publication Data

A Taste of East Anglia
Julia Skinner

The Francis Frith Collection®
Frith's Barn, Teffont,
Salisbury, Wiltshire SP3 5QP
Tel: +44 (0) 1722 716 376
Email: info@francisfrith.co.uk
www.francisfrith.com

Printed and bound in England

Front Cover: Sudbury, The Market 1904 51156t
The colour-tinting in this image is for illustrative purposes only, and is not intended
to be historically accurate.

Every attempt has been made to contact copyright holders of illustrative material.
We will be happy to give full acknowledgement in future editions for any items not
credited. Any information should be directed to The Francis Frith Collection.

As with any historical database, the Francis Frith archive is constantly being
corrected and improved, and the publishers would welcome information on
omissions or inaccuracies.

CONTENTS

INTRODUCTION

Travel around the counties of East Anglia through the pages of this book and discover a selection of the delicious traditional food of the area, as well as some of the stories and fascinating facts behind the recipes. Your journey will be given added savour by the historical images taken by photographers from The Francis Frith Collection, showing the people and places of East Anglia in the past.

Regional traditional dishes were developed from the local produce that was available to thrifty housewives who had to feed large, hungry families on a limited budget. Many of the old recipes also reflect the limited cookery techniques that were available in the past, as well as the skills of the cooks who were able to provide cheap and tasty meals with only a fire, a skillet and a cauldron to cook with, often producing the historical version of 'boil in the bag' meals.

This book is not intended to provide a comprehensive collection of the local recipes of the region, and some recipes are modern interpretations using some of the fine local produce that the area is famous for, but we hope that the food described within these pages, as well as the descriptions of traditional customs, sayings and local dialect words, will provide you with a taste of East Anglia.

Lowestoft, London Road North 1896 37924

SOUPS AND SNACKS

RECIPE

—.—

Essex Pea Soup

Peas are cultivated on a large scale throughout East Anglia. Pea pods have an intense flavour, and this recipe ensures that this is not wasted.

450g/1 lb fresh peas in their pods
1 onion
50g/2oz butter
900ml/1½ pints good ham or vegetable stock
1 teaspoonful of sugar
2 sprigs of fresh mint
1 teaspoonful of cornflour
300ml/ ½ pint milk
Salt and pepper

Shell the peas, wash the empty pods and remove the stringy edge and any other hard, fibrous bits. Peel and finely chop the onion. Melt the butter in a large heavy saucepan, add the peas, pods and chopped onion and fry gently for a few minutes until softened. Add the stock, sugar and sprigs of mint. Bring to the boil, then reduce heat, cover and simmer until the peas and pods are tender. Blend the cornflour with a little milk and stir it into the soup, together with the remaining milk. Increase the heat and bring the soup back to the boil, stirring all the time. Remove from heat and allow to cool for a few minutes, then liquidise the soup in a blender or pass it through a sieve. Season the soup with salt and pepper to taste, and reheat before serving.

—.—

Stilton Cheese

Stilton is a small village south of Peterborough with a reputation for a cheese which it has never produced. The village was an important staging point on the Great North Road. Leicestershire farmers took their produce to the 17th-century Bell Inn for delivery by coach to London, where the cheese became known as Stilton. Even so, each year there is a cheese-rolling charity race along the village, with local teams, many in fancy dress, bowling a 'cheese' (usually a log cut and painted to resemble a cheese) along the High Street. The winning team receives a crate of beer and a real cheese.

St Ives, Old River 1914 66958

RECIPE

—·—

Celery and Stilton Soup

Celery is an important crop around Ely in Cambridgeshire, where it grows well in the rich, black Fenland soil.

> 40g/1½ oz butter
> 1 onion, finely chopped
> 1 potato, cut into small cubes
> 1 whole head of celery, thinly sliced
> 900ml/1½ pints good chicken or vegetable stock
> 115g/4oz Stilton cheese, crumbled
> 150ml/ ¼ pint single cream
> Salt and freshly ground black pepper

Melt the butter in a large pan. Add the onion and cook over a medium heat for 5 minutes until it is transparent. Add the potato and celery and cook for a further 5 minutes until the vegetables begin to soften and brown. Add the stock, bring to the boil, then reduce heat, cover the pan and simmer for 30-40 minutes, until the vegetables are very soft. Allow to cool for a few minutes, then liquidise the soup in a blender, or pass it through a sieve, then return it to the pan and season to taste. Heat the soup through to just below the boil, then remove the pan from the heat, add the cheese and stir until it has melted. Stir in the cream and reheat just before serving, being careful not to allow the soup to boil.

—·—

Pin Mill, The Butt and Oyster1909 62001

RECIPE

—. —

Huntingdon Stuffed Pears

2 large ripe pears
115g/4oz Stilton cheese, firm but not hard
25g/1oz soft butter
1 tablespoonful double cream
Freshly ground black pepper
25g/1oz walnuts, finely chopped, plus 4 walnut halves
4 crisp lettuce leaves
2 tablespoons lemon juice

Peel, halve and core the pears, hollowing them out carefully. Cream together the cheese, butter, cream and black pepper, using either a blender or a bowl and wooden spoon. Add the chopped walnuts. Fill the centres of the pears with the mixture and stand each on a lettuce leaf on small plates. Put a half-walnut in the centre of each. Squeeze lemon juice over the unfilled parts of the pears to prevent them from discolouring, and serve as soon as possible after preparing.

—. —

Shellfish

Shellfish thrive around the East Anglian coast. Cromer is famous for its crabs and Wells-next-the-Sea is known for the quality of the locally-caught whelks. Cockles are dredged from the sands around Leigh-on-Sea and Southend, among other places, and the small village of Stiffkey in Norfolk is famous for the blue-shelled cockles known as 'Stookey (or Stewkey) Blues'. The Wells whelkers were renowned along the Norfolk coast for their persistence in pursuing their trade. Whelking was not always a comfortable affair. Dropping pots from open clinker-built boats in pitch darkness and foul weather meant the whelkers could often find themselves stranded for hours on end on the wrong side of the bar waiting for the tide.

Wells-next-the-Sea, Bringing in the Whelks 1929 82003

RECIPE

—.—

Angels on Horseback

Colchester has been at the heart of the oyster trade in Britain for many years, and the oyster season is opened by a traditional festival when the Mayor, civic dignitaries and members of the Fishing Board go by boat to Pyfleet Creek, where the oyster fattening beds lie. Here the loyal toast is drunk, gingerbread and gin are consumed, and the Mayor makes the first ceremonial oyster dredge of the season; the gingerbread is traditional and may be an echo of the offerings given to the local sea god in ancient times. This recipe makes a delicious snack or appetizer. It dates back to Victorian times, when oysters were both plentiful and cheap, an everyday dish that everyone could afford.

> 16 oysters, removed from their shells
> Fresh lemon juice
> 8 rashers of streaky bacon with their rinds removed
> 8 small slices of bread
> Butter
> Paprika, or a dash of Tabasco sauce (optional)

Pre-heat the oven to 200°C/400°C/Gas Mark 6.

Sprinkle each oyster with a little lemon juice. Lay the bacon rashers on a board, slide the back of a knife along each one to stretch it and then cut it in half crosswise. Wrap a piece of bacon around each oyster and secure with a wooden cocktail stick. Arrange the bacon-wrapped oysters on a baking sheet. Put the oysters and bacon into the pre-heated hot oven and cook for 8-10 minutes. Whilst the bacon and oysters are cooking, toast the bread. When the bacon is cooked through, spread each slice of hot toast with butter, and place a bacon-wrapped oyster on top of each piece. Sprinkle with a little paprika or a dash of Tabasco sauce, if used, before serving.

—.—

Sheringham, Fishermen Mending Crab Pots 1906 56879

Southend-on-Sea, The Pier 1898 41377

RECIPE

Cockles and Bacon

This is a favourite way of eating cockles in Norfolk.

600ml/1 pint (volume) fresh cockles
8 rashers of streaky bacon
A little oil or lard for frying
Bread slices for toast
Butter

Wash the cockles thoroughly in plenty of cold water, or leave them to soak for several hours if possible. Bring a large saucepan of water to the boil. Place the cockles in the water and leave for a few minutes, until their shells have opened. Remove from heat, strain and leave the cockles to cool. When they have cooled, pick the cockles out of their shells. Fry the bacon rashers in a little oil or lard until they are crisp, then remove from the pan and keep warm. Add the cockles to the pan and toss them in the bacon fat until they are lightly browned. Serve the cockles and bacon on slices of hot buttered toast.

Aldeburgh, The Old Ionia 1952 A28001

Weaver's Beef

Sprats are caught along the East Anglian coast, and Aldeburgh and Southwold are particularly famous for these small fish, a small cousin of the herring. The first sprats of the season used to be sent from Aldeburgh to London for the Lord Mayor's Banquet. In olden times sprats were caught in such large numbers off the East Anglian coast and were so inexpensive that in Colchester, where many people were employed in the textile industry, they were known as 'weaver's beef'. Sprats are cooked like whitebait, coated in seasoned flour or oatmeal and then fried until crisp.

Southwold, From the Pier 1906 56829

RECIPE

Crispy Fried Whitebait

Whitebait are the tiny silver fry (young) of sprats or herrings, and are eaten whole, fried until crisp. The whitebait harvest was important to Southend in past years, and small quantities of this fish are still landed here. A special service takes place every year at the end of Southend Pier to bless the first catch of the season, which is followed by a Whitebait Lunch and then a Whitebait Festival.

> 450g/11b whitebait
> 25g/1oz plain flour
> Salt and pepper
> Oil for deep frying
> Lemon wedges

Wash and dry the whitebait. Season the flour with salt and pepper, and toss the whitebait in the seasoned flour a few at a time, until each fish is coated. Heat the oil in a large pan or deep fryer until it is just smoking. Add a small batch of whitebait and fry for 2-3 minutes, until they are crisp and golden brown. Lift out, drain and keep hot whilst the rest of the fish are fried. Sprinkle the cooked whitebait with salt, and serve with lemon wedges and slices of brown bread and butter.

FISH

The herring trade made the fortunes of several East Anglian coastal towns, particularly Great Yarmouth and Lowestoft. By the end of the 19th century Great Yarmouth was the leading herring port in the world. During the season, which lasted about ten weeks from the end of September, the town's population would be swelled by thousands of fishermen with their wives and daughters who gutted and packed the fish, and also by coopers who made the barrels the fish were transported in. Herrings were also dried and cured into the famous Great Yarmouth kippers.

In the 1860s, fishermen from Scotland started to arrive in the area. They brought with them a method for pickling the fish in brine, rather than the traditional method of smoking, which produced the Yarmouth bloater. So popular was it that pickled herring overtook smoked herring in popularity by the turn of the century. Yarmouth's fishing industry continued during the first half of the 20th century, but by the mid 1950s it was clear that fish stocks were seriously depleted. By the time they were sold in the early 1960s Yarmouth's fleet of fishing boats had dwindled to six, and the town's herring fleet is no more.

Lowestoft was particularly famous for herring and mackerel fishing. By the 1880s Lowestoft was estimated to have had 312 drifters and 139 trawlers. The herring season lasted from September to November, during which time every available space in the town was used to process the herrings. Gutting, pickling and packing were done by women – mainly Scots – who followed the Scottish fishing boats down the coast. Their hands were bandaged to protect them against the salt and brine, and as they were on piece-rate, it was essential to keep their fingers nimble. This they did by continuously knitting in their free time. Herring fishery in Lowestoft lasted until 1966 – a year later the herring shoals had all but disappeared, the victims of over-fishing.

Great Yarmouth, Fish Market c1900 G56503

Great Yarmouth, Scottish Fishing Boats c1900 G56507

RECIPE

Herrings with Mustard Sauce

Herrings are highly nutritious and were a staple part of the diet in Victorian times. Here, the herrings are served with a savoury stuffing for a tasty lunch or supper. The mustard sauce is a reminder of Norfolk's famous mustard industry – bright yellow fields of mustard have been grown in the county ever since Jeremiah Colman opened his first mustard mill near Norwich 1814 and started making his condiment.

4 large herrings	Mustard Sauce
3 heaped tablespoonfuls fresh white breadcrumbs	40g/1½ oz butter
	25g/1oz plain flour
1 heaped teaspoonful finely chopped parsley	450ml/ ¾ pint milk
	Salt and black pepper
A squeeze of lemon juice	1 level tablespoonful dry Norfolk mustard powder
Grated rind of half a lemon	
Salt and black pepper	1 tablespoonful wine vinegar
Oil for frying	1 level teaspoonful caster sugar
25g/1oz butter	Lemon wedges and fresh parsley sprigs for garnish

Remove the heads from the herrings, clean, gut and bone them. Wash the herrings and pat them thoroughly dry. Put the breadcrumbs, parsley, lemon juice and lemon rind in a basin; season lightly with salt and freshly ground black pepper.

Melt the butter and stir into the breadcrumbs to bind the mixture, which should now be moist, but crumbly. Stuff the herrings with the breadcrumb mixture, and if necessary secure them with wooden cocktail sticks. Slash the skins crossways two or three times on each side; brush the herrings with oil and wrap each in foil. Put the herrings in a well-buttered deep baking dish; cover with lightly buttered greaseproof paper and bake in the centre of a pre-heated oven at 200°C/400°F/Gas Mark 6 for 35-40 minutes.

For the sauce, melt 25g/1oz of the butter in a pan; stir in the flour and cook for 1 minute. Gradually stir in the milk, beating well until the sauce is quite smooth. Bring to the boil and simmer for 2-3 minutes; season with salt and pepper. Blend the mustard powder with the vinegar and stir into the sauce; add the sugar. Check seasoning and stir in the remaining butter.

Transfer the baked herrings to a hot serving dish and garnish with wedges of lemon and sprigs of parsley. Serve the mustard sauce separately.

Cromer, The Lifeboat 1922 72651

Devil light the fire!

Legend says that disaster followed the lighting of an oven in Peterborough in 1116, when a major fire destroyed the monastery buildings and the church. Traditionally the fire was said to have been caused when a monk, struggling to light the bake-house oven, cursed it and cried: 'Devil light the fire!'.
In 1118 work began on a new church, the present cathedral.

Peterborough, The Cathedral, the Slype
1919 69085

RECIPE

—·—

Kipper Savoury

2 large kippers
50g/2oz butter
1 tablespoonful of chopped chives
½ clove of garlic crushed with a few
grains of salt

<u>For the pastry</u>
225g/8oz plain flour
75g/3oz lard or margarine
75g/3oz peeled and grated raw
  potato
About 1 tablespoonful cold water

<u>To finish</u>
A little melted butter

Pre-heat the oven to 200°C/400°F/Gas Mark 6.

Simmer the kipper fillets in boiling water until the flesh comes away from the bones easily; alternatively, steam the kippers between two plates over a pan of simmering water for about 20 minutes. Remove flesh, and discard the bones and skin. Soften the butter gently in a basin, but do not let it melt to oil. Add the flaked kipper flesh, the chopped chives and crushed garlic, and mix well. Rub the lard or margarine into the flour, add the grated potato and mix it all to a firm dough with a little water. Roll out half the dough and line a pie plate about 20 cm (7-8 inches) in diameter. Spread the filling on to the pastry, not quite to the edge, and dampen the edge of the pastry with cold water. Roll out the remaining dough and use it to make a cover, press the edges together to seal well, and trim and flute the edge. Using the tip of a sharp knife, make a criss-cross pattern on top of the pie, cutting through the lid to the filling, to resemble a fishing net. Brush the top of the pastry with melted butter, and bake in a pre-heated oven at 200°C/400°F/Gas Mark 6 for about 35 minutes, until the pastry is crisp and golden. This is good served with parsley sauce.

—·—

Thaxted, Post Office 1906 55463

Cambridgeshire Dialect Words

'Mizzle' - mist.

'Dockey' - the mid-day snack at work. It possibly gets its name from when wages were 'docked' for the time that workers took off for their meal break.

'Slubby' - runny mud.

'Ockered' - awkward or contrary.

'Backerds' - backwards.

Maldon, A Barge at Beeleigh 1906 55547x

Eels

This photograph (below) shows an eel catcher's hut in the Norfolk Broads – notice the nets to the left of the hut. Eels used to be commonly found in the rivers of the Broads, but there is now only one eel catcher's hut remaining, at Kendal Dyke above Potter Heigham.

Eels were once so common in the fenland area of Cambridgeshire that they became a form of currency known as 'booklets' or 'sticks' of eels, with which land rent could be paid to the Church or State. One 'stick' comprised 25 eels. The monks at Ely exchanged 4,000 eels a year for the stone to build Ely Cathedral.

The Broads, An Eel Catcher's Hut c1945 T213015

RECIPE

—·—

Eel Pie

1.4kg/3lbs skinned eels
300ml/ ½ pint fish stock
Salt and pepper
A pinch of mixed herbs
115g/4oz sliced onions
1 tablespoonful lemon juice
225g/8oz shortcrust pastry
1 egg

Cut the eels into small pieces and place them in a pan. Add the fish stock, salt and pepper, herbs and onions; simmer gently until the eel pieces are tender enough for the bones to be removed. Arrange the boned eels in a pie dish, and add the lemon juice and enough strained stock to cover the eels. Cover with pastry; brush with beaten egg and bake in a hot oven for about 45 minutes (225°C/425°F/Gas Mark 6). A little extra stock may be poured into the pie through a hole in the centre of the pastry before serving.

—·—

MEAT, GAME AND POULTRY

Maldon, Butchers, High Street 1906 55544x

Crystal Sea Salt

Maldon is situated on the River Blackwater, one of the saltiest rivers in England. A crystal sea salt, which has a more pronounced flavour than ordinary salt, has been produced here for many centuries.

Maldon, The Promenade 1909 62098

Essex dialect words

'Barmed' - dirtied with mud.

'Clung' - lumps of wet mud or freshly dug earth.

'Dodman' - a name for a snail, and thus used for a low or lazy person or animal.

'Gant', or 'gantway' - an alleyway between houses.

'Pollywags' - tadpoles.

'Rooning' - gathering mushrooms.

'Slud'- sludgy mud.

'Sobbled' - soaked, as in wet clothes.

'Venturemous' - bold, brave.

Chelmsford, High Street 1895 35514

RECITE

Steak and Oyster Hotpot

450g/1 lb braising steak
50g/2oz lard
2 lambs' kidneys
12 shelled oysters
1 onion
25g/1oz flour
600ml/1 pint water
675g/1 ½ lbs potatoes
Salt and pepper

Cut the steak into small cubes about 1cm (½ inch) square. Melt the lard in a large pan, and brown the pieces of meat a few pieces at a time. Transfer the browned meat to a casserole dish.

Skin and slice the kidneys and add to the meat in the dish. Add the oysters, reserving any liquor to use in the sauce. Peel and slice the potatoes, and use them to cover the meat and oysters in the dish. Peel and slice the onions and gently fry them in the remaining fat in the pan until they are transparent. Sprinkle the flour over the onions, stir in and cook gently for a few minutes. Gradually add in the water and oyster liquor, stirring all the time. Bring to the boil until the sauce thickens, stirring all the time. When the sauce has thickened, season to taste and pour it over the meat in the casserole. Cover the casserole with its lid and cook in a moderate oven (180°C/350°C/Gas Mark 4) for 1½ hours. Then remove the lid and continue to cook for a further 30 minutes, so that the potatoes brown and crisp.

RECIPE

—·—

Suffolk Stew

Suffolk's rich pastures provide quality beef and lamb. Order the best end of lamb chined from the butcher, and begin preparations a day in advance for this hearty, satisfying stew.

1 best end of lamb
50g/2oz lentils
25g/1oz haricot beans
25g/1oz pearl barley
2 large potatoes
1 large turnip
4 carrots
4 onions
2 bay leaves
½ level teaspoonful salt
½ level teaspoonful black pepper
1 clove garlic
1 level teaspoonful mixed herbs

Soak the lentils, haricot beans and pearl barley in cold water overnight. The following day, peel and roughly chop all the vegetables; put them in a large saucepan. Trim any excess fat from the best end of lamb and cut the meat into single chops. Add these, together with the bay leaves, salt, pepper, crushed garlic and herbs to the vegetables.

Drain the lentils, haricot beans and pearl barley, before adding them to the pan. Pour over 1.8 litres (3 pints) of water, cover the pan with a lid and bring to the boil. Simmer gently for 3 hours. When ready to eat, spoon the stew into a warm serving dish.

—·—

RECIPE

Honey Roasted Turkey with Candied Potatoes

It is widely considered that the best poultry in the country comes from Norfolk, which is especially renowned for the quality of its turkeys. In the 17th century flocks of the famous Norfolk Black turkeys were driven on foot from Norfolk to London for the Christmas markets, in great droves of 500 birds or more. The journey took about 3 months. An annual turkey fair was held at Attleborough, and Daniel Defoe recorded in the early 18th century that each year 300 droves of Norfolk turkeys went through the town of Stratford St Mary in Suffolk on their way to London.

This is a Norfolk recipe for cooking turkey, which also produces delicious potatoes, candied from the honey in the pan. The gravy to accompany the turkey should be made separately, as the honey in the pan will make it too sweet if the cooking juices are used in the usual way.

> 225g/8oz honey
> 115g/4oz butter
> 3.5-5.5kg/8-12 lbs turkey
> 1.4kg/3 lb potatoes, peeled and halved

Allow a total cooking time of 15 minutes roasting per 450g (1 lb) weight of the turkey.

Gently melt the honey and butter together in a pan and stir well to mix it. Place the turkey in a roasting tin and pour the honey and butter mixture all over it. Allow the turkey to stand for an hour or so, basting occasionally with the mixture which has run off into the tray.

Pre-heat the oven to 200°C/400°F/Gas Mark 6.

Arrange the potatoes around the turkey, place the roasting tin in the pre-heated oven and cook for 40 minutes. The honey will make an almost black crust over the bird, sealing in the flavour. After 40 minutes, baste the turkey with the mixture that has run off into the tin and turn the potatoes, reduce the oven heat to 180°C/350°F/Gas Mark 4 and cook for a further 30 minutes. Baste the turkey and turn the potatoes again, then cover the roasting tin with foil and continue to cook in accordance with the time scale above.

Remove the foil for the last 15 minutes of cooking time to allow the skin to crisp.

MEAT, GAME AND POULTRY

Bury St Edmunds, Cornhill 1898 41246

37

The Dunmow Flitch Trials

The event known as the Dunmow Flitch now takes place every four years in the Essex town of Dunmow, in which a flitch of bacon – a whole side of a pig – is presented to a married couple who have not, in the past 366 days, 'offended each other in deed or in word', nor in any way regretted their marriage. The event dates from very early medieval times: Langland mentions it in 'The Vision of Piers Plowman', and Chaucer in 'The Wife of Bath's Tale'.

The event was allowed to lapse in the 18th century, but was revived in 1855 and has continued ever since. Now known as the Dunmow Flitch Trials, the ceremony involves tongue-in-cheek court officials and a jury of 'six maidens and six bachelors'. A Judge assesses the claims of the vying couples, and claimants are quizzed on various aspects of their nuptial harmony.

In the 2000 Flitch Trials, the flitch was awarded to four couples. This photograph (left) shows Fred and Joan Shepherd being carried in a replica of the ancient Flitch Chair.

Great Dunmow, Flitch Trials, Chairing the Winners 2000
D90705

Central to the ceremony is the flitch of bacon itself. Here it is (right), hung from a frame and draped with greenery.

These photographs of the Flitch Trials were taken by a local photographer, Mike Perry of David Lipson Photography, who has actually won the Flitch himself.

Great Dunmow, The Flitch Trials
2000 D90706

RECIPE

Fidget Pie

Fidget (or fitchet) pies made with bacon, onions and apples are popular in East Anglia.

For the pastry:
175g/6oz plain flour
75g/3oz butter or margarine
Pinch of salt

For the filling:
2 onions
450g/1 lb cooking apples
450g/1 lb back bacon
Salt and pepper
150ml/ ¼ pint cider
Beaten egg or milk to glaze

Pre-heat the oven to 220°C/425°F/Gas Mark 7.

Peel and finely chop the onions. Peel, core and slice the apples. Cut the bacon into small pieces. Put the onions, apples and bacon into a pie dish, season to taste with salt and pepper, and pour the cider over. Sieve the flour and salt into a bowl, and rub in the butter or margarine until the mixture resembles fine breadcrumbs. Add enough cold water to make a soft dough. (The pastry can be made in a food processor if preferred). Roll out the pastry on a floured board, and place it on top of the pie dish – use a pie funnel in the centre of the dish if you have one, to prevent the pie lid from caving in. Pinch the pastry edge around the pie dish to seal, and trim. Brush the pastry with the beaten egg or milk to glaze. Bake in the hot pre-heated oven for 20 minutes, then reduce the heat to 180°C/350°F/Gas Mark 4 and cook for a further 30 minutes, until the pastry is crisp and golden.

East Dereham 1893 33308

RECIPE

— · —

Norfolk Plough Pudding

225g/8oz self-raising flour
115g/4oz shredded suet
450g/1 lb pork sausage meat
115g/4oz streaky bacon
1 onion
1 tablespoonful chopped sage
Salt and pepper

Grease a 1.15 litre (2 pint) pudding bowl. Mix together the flour and suet, a pinch of salt, and enough cold water to bind it all together into a firm dough. Roll out the dough on a floured surface and use two-thirds of it to line the pudding bowl. Mix together the sausage meat, chopped bacon, onion and sage, and season with salt and pepper. Press the meat mixture into the pudding bowl, and use the remaining pastry to make a lid, sealing the edges together well.

Cover the pudding bowl with pleated greaseproof paper and a piece of foil, and tie down well. Place the pudding bowl in a large saucepan of boiling water and cover with the saucepan lid. Steam for 4 hours, topping up the saucepan with more boiling water from time to time to ensure that the pan does not boil dry. When cooked, turn out the pudding onto a warm serving dish and serve piping hot.

— · —

A Taste of EAST ANGLIA

Coltishall 1902 48127X

RECIPE

Ongar Ham Cake

675g/1½ lbs cooked ham
150ml/ ¼ pint ale or beer
A large slice of thick white bread
1 egg
Salt and pepper

Pre-heat the oven to 200°C/400°F/Gas Mark 6.

Remove the crust from the slice of bread. Place the bread in a bowl with the ale or beer and leave until the bread is thoroughly soaked. Finely mince the ham, add the soaked bread and mix well together. Season the mixture with salt and pepper, add the egg and beat it all together. Lightly wet a mould or pudding basin and put in the mixture, pressing it down gently, and firm the top. Bake in the pre-heated oven for about 1 hour, or until it is set and well-coloured. When cooked, turn out the cake on to a warm serving dish if it is to be eaten hot. The cake can also be eaten cold, in which case leave it in the mould or basin to cool and firm up before turning out.

St Ives, Cromwell Statue 1901 48069

RECIPE

Cromwell's Favourite

This recipe for veal with orange is said to have been Oliver Cromwell's favourite dish. Cromwell was born in Huntingdon in 1599 and was educated at the Grammar School in the town, before becoming MP for Cambridge and ultimately Lord Protector of England, Scotland and Ireland after the Civil War.

> 1.75-2.25kg/4-5 lbs breast of veal, boned
> 115g/4oz fresh white breadcrumbs
> 50g/2oz raisins
> 50g/2oz currants
> 50g/2oz shredded beef suet
> Salt and freshly ground black pepper
> Ground nutmeg
> 2 large oranges
> 1 large egg yolk
> 50g/2oz lard
> 25g/1oz cornflour
> Caster sugar
> 6 tablespoonfuls claret

Pre-heat the oven to 200°/400°F/Gas Mark 6.

First, make the stuffing: mix the breadcrumbs, raisins, currants, suet and a pinch of salt, pepper and nutmeg together in a bowl. Finely grate the rind from the oranges and add to the mixture with the lightly beaten egg yolk. Stir in just enough cold water to bind the mixture. Spread the stuffing mixture over the boned veal, then roll up the meat and tie it with string at 2cm (1 inch) intervals. Put the roll of meat into a roasting tin, add the lard and roast for 2½ hours in the centre of the pre-heated oven. Baste the meat occasionally, and cover with foil if it browns too quickly. When the meat is cooked, place it on a serving dish and keep it warm in the oven while the sauce is prepared. Skim all the fat from the juices in the roasting tin and heat them in a small saucepan. Blend the cornflour with 1 tablespoonful of cold water and add it to the juices, stirring continuously until the sauce has thickened. Bring to the boil and season to taste with salt, freshly ground black pepper, sugar and ground nutmeg. Stir in the claret, reduce the heat and simmer the sauce gently. Remove the remaining rind and pith from the oranges and cut the flesh into small pieces. Add the orange pieces to the sauce and heat it gently. When ready to serve, cut the veal into thick slices and serve with the sauce.

RECIPE

—·—

Autumn Rabbit and Norfolk Dumplings

In previous centuries Norfolk was overrun with rabbits. When farm workers 'lived in' on the farms, rabbits formed a large part of their diet and were known as 'hollow meat'. In fact, some farmworkers got so bored of eating rabbit that a proviso had to be made that they should only be fed 'hollow meat' for a certain number of days a week.

> 1 rabbit, jointed
> 25g/1oz lard
> 25g/1oz plain flour
> 300ml/ ½ pint ale or beer
> 1 onion
> 1 carrot
> 1 large apple
> 50g/2oz button mushrooms
> A sprig each of fresh parsley and thyme
> 1 bay leaf
> Salt and pepper

Oven temperature: 180°C/350°F/Gas Mark 4.

Melt the lard in a large heavy pan, add the rabbit joints and brown them. Remove the rabbit from the pan and place in a casserole dish. Stir the flour into the hot fat in the pan, cook for a few minutes, then add the ale or beer a little at a time, stirring continuously until the sauce thickens. Pour the sauce over the rabbit joints in the casserole. Peel and slice the onion, carrot and apple, and add to the casserole. Chop the mushrooms and herbs and add to the casserole, together with the bay leaf. Season with salt and pepper. Cover the casserole dish with its lid, and cook in a moderate oven for about 2 hours, until the rabbit is tender. Remove the bay leaf before serving.

Put the Norfolk Dumplings (see recipe opposite) on top of the casserole for the last 25-30 minutes of the cooking time.

—·—

RECIPE

Norfolk Dumplings

In Norfolk, dumplings cooked on top of a stew are called 'floaters' or 'swimmers'. They are light, and do not contain suet (heavy suet dumplings are known disparagingly in Norfolk as 'sinkers'). There is some argument as to whether Norfolk dumplings should contain yeast or not – although there is a version made with yeast, like a bread dough, a recipe for the non-yeast version is given here.

Allow 1 heaped tablespoonful of self-raising flour per person (or use plain flour and 1 teaspoonful of baking powder), a pinch of salt and water to mix. Sieve the flour and salt into a bowl. Add sufficient water to make a light dough. Turn out onto a floured surface, knead lightly, then divide into the required amount of pieces and form into round dumplings. Place them on top of the casserole for the last 25-30 minutes of cooking time.

Old Michaelmas Day

The calendar changes of 1752 officially moved Michaelmas Day to 29th September, but in Suffolk roast goose continued to be the traditional dish eaten for dinner on 'Old Michaelmas Day' (11th October). There was a saying that if you ate eat goose on this day, you would have no money worries for the following year:

'Whoever eats goose on Michaelmas Day
Shall never lack money for his debts to pay.'

RECImPE

~ . ~

Roast Wild Duck

The Broads area of Norfolk is particularly known for the variety of wildfowl to be found there. Both wild duck and geese formed an important part of the local diet in past times. Wild duck, such as mallard, teal and widgeon, should not be overcooked – allow a roasting time of between 30-50 minutes, depending on the size of the bird.

> 1 wild duck
> A knob of butter
> Orange juice
>
> For the sauce:
> 1 tablespoonful of lemon juice
> 1 tablespoonful of sugar
> 2 tablespoonfuls of port wine
> 1 tablespoonful of tomato ketchup
> Salt
> Cayenne pepper

Pre-heat the oven to 190°C/375°F/Gas Mark 5.

Put the duck in a roasting tin. Place a knob of butter inside the duck, and pour some orange juice over the bird. Roast in the pre-heated oven for about 30-50 minutes (depending on the size of the bird) until it is tender, basting occasionally with the juices in the tin. When the duck is cooked, mix all the sauce ingredients together and pour over the bird before serving.

~ . ~

Horstead, The Mill 1902 48149

Suffolk Dialect Words

'Airy-wiggle' - an earwig.

'Hoistes' - trousers that are too short.

'Lummox' - a clumsy person.

'Coupla three' - two or three.

'Arter' - after.

'Biddy' - old woman, widow.

'Dwile' - cloth (from the Dutch word 'dweil').

'Mawther' - a young girl.

'Wholly' - very.

Southwold, Characters 1891 28352x

Jubilee Feast

In 1897 the Diamond Jubilee of Queen Victoria was celebrated in Norwich with fireworks and the distribution of beef and mutton from Australia. The Mayor hosted a dinner for over a thousand poor people in St Andrew's Hall, a precursor of the present tradition in the city of giving a free meal on Christmas Day to the poor and homeless at the same venue.

Norwich, Market Place 1929 81796

VEGETABLE AND SUPPER DISHES

Poor Man's Asparagus

Asparagus is widely cultivated in East Anglia, but a wild plant, often called 'Poor Man's Asparagus', is also popular. Marsh Samphire, or glasswort, grows on salt marshes around the coast of Norfolk and Suffolk, and the green fleshy tips can be eaten raw or lightly cooked in salads, or hot with butter or with fish. Samphire is often known as 'poor man's asparagus', but is also enjoyed by the rich – it was served at the royal wedding breakfast of Prince Charles and Lady Diana Spencer in 1981, as a symbol of Sandringham in Norfolk, where the royal family has a residence.

Cambridge, Petty Cury 1909 61469

RECIPE

Buttered Asparagus

East Anglia is famous for its asparagus, which is in season from May to early July.

450g/1 lb asparagus spears
25g/1oz butter
1 teaspoonful caster sugar
Salt and pepper

Cook the asparagus in a pan of lightly salted water for about 5-6 minutes, then drain well. Melt the butter and fry the asparagus gently for a further 5 minutes. Sprinkle the sugar over the asparagus, season with salt and pepper, and serve.

Walberswick, Fruit and Veg Stall 1919 69128x

RECIPE

— . —

Cambridge Cabbage and Bacon

1 large crisp white cabbage

4 rashers of back bacon

4 rashers of streaky bacon

A knob of butter

Salt, pepper and a pinch of ground allspice

Trim and quarter the cabbage and wash it well. Bring a large pan of salted water to the boil and add the cabbage. While it is cooking, cut the bacon into small pieces, and fry in butter in a hot frying pan. When it is tender, after about 10 minutes, drain the cabbage thoroughly, cut it into shreds with a knife and press lightly to strain off the water. Place it in a mound on a deep dish and throw the bacon and its hot fat over the top. Season with pepper and a pinch of allspice.

— . —

RECIPE

— · —

Suffolk Red Cabbage

This dish has a delicious sharp-sweet flavour that goes extremely well with game, roast pork or sausages.

> 1 red cabbage
> 50g/2oz butter
> 1 slice of ham, thickly cut – weighing about 115g/4oz
> 2 tablespoonfuls vinegar
> 1 tablespoonful sugar
> Salt and pepper

Cut the red cabbage into quarters with a stainless steel knife; remove the cores, then slice fairly thin. Melt the butter in an ovenproof casserole and add the ham cut in little sticks about 3cm (1 inch) long. Let it simmer gently in the butter without browning for five minutes, then stir in the sliced cabbage and turn it over in the butter until it is all coated and glistening. Cover the pan and allow to sweat for 10 minutes. Stir in the vinegar and sugar, season with salt and pepper and cover the pan. Put in a very low oven, 160°C/325°F/Gas Mark 3, and let it cook very gently for 2 hours, stirring occasionally. This reheats well.

— · —

RECIPE

Suffolk Carrot Pie

This tasty dish should be served hot, and also makes a good accompaniment to cold meats.

6 carrots, grated
6 potatoes, peeled and grated
2 eggs, separated
Salt and pepper
2 tablespoonfuls of plain flour

Pre-heat the oven to 180°C/350°F/Gas Mark 4.

Grease an ovenproof dish. Beat the egg yolks in a bowl and season with salt and pepper. Gradually stir in the flour to make a smooth paste, and mix the grated carrots and potatoes into the mixture. Beat the egg whites until they form stiff peaks, and carefully fold them into the mixture. Turn it all into the greased dish, and bake in the pre-heated oven until the pie is golden brown.

Great Yarmouth, Boys in Regent Road 1896 37959v

PUDDINGS, PIES AND DESSERTS

Ipswich, The Docks 1893 32208

RECIPE

—·—

Ipswich Almond Pudding

450ml/15fl oz milk
150ml/5fl oz double cream
50g/2oz fresh white breadcrumbs
75g/3oz caster sugar
175g/6oz ground almonds
1 teaspoonful orange flower or rose water
    (available from chemists)
3 beaten eggs
25g/1oz butter

Pre-heat the oven to 180°C/350°F/Gas Mark 4.

Place the milk in a saucepan and heat until warmed. Place the breadcrumbs in a large mixing bowl, and pour the warm milk over them. Mix in the sugar, almonds and orange or rose water and leave to soak for 15 minutes. Add the beaten eggs to the breadcrumb mixture and mix well. Pour the mixture into a buttered pie dish. Place the dish in a deep roasting tin with enough hot water to come half way up the sides of the pie dish. Bake in a pre-heated oven until set (180°C/350°F/Gas Mark 4). Serve hot with cream or custard.

—·—

RECIPE

—.—

Burnt Cambridge Cream

The recipe for Cambridge Burnt Cream is supposed to have originated at Trinity College in the 19th century.

> 600ml/1 pint double cream
> 1 teaspoonful vanilla essence
> 4 egg yolks
> 3 tablespoonfuls sugar

Put the cream and vanilla essence in a saucepan and bring to the boil; meanwhile, in a large mixing bowl beat the egg yolks with 1 tablespoonful of the sugar until they are thick and pale yellow. Remove the cream from the heat and allow to cool slightly, then pour it steadily over the egg yolks, whisking constantly. Transfer the mixture to an ovenproof dish or individual ramekins. Bake at 150°C/300°F/Gas Mark 2 for about 30 minutes, until set. Leave to cool, then refrigerate for several hours.

About two hours before serving, pre-heat the grill to its highest temperature. Sprinkle the remaining sugar thickly and evenly over the surface of the cooked cream. Place the dish or ramekins under the grill, as close to the heat as possible, and allow the sugar to caramelise until a rich brown colour, but watching carefully to make sure that the sugar does not actually burn. Cool, and chill in the refrigerator again before serving so that the topping goes crunchy.

—.—

Cambridge, The Cam, Trinity Bridge 1914 66902a

RECIPE

—.—

Fen Country Apple Cake

750g/1½ lbs cooking apples
Juice of half a lemon
25g/1oz butter or margarine
50g/2oz caster sugar
2 rounded tablespoonfuls of semolina
225g/8oz shortcrust or puff pastry
25g/1oz currants
3 tablespoonfuls of black treacle

Peel, core and slice the apples. Put the apples, lemon juice and butter into a pan, cover, and simmer slowly until pulpy. Add the sugar and semolina, and bring slowly to the boil. Cook gently for five minutes or until the mixture has thickened. Remove from the heat and leave until completely cold.

Divide the pastry into two pieces. Roll out one portion and use to line an 18-20cm (7-8 inch) heatproof plate. Spread with half the apple filling to within half an inch of the edges. Sprinkle with currants and add the treacle, and then top with the remaining filling. Roll out the rest of the pastry into a 22-24cm (9 inch) round, moisten the edges with water and cover the pie. Press the edges well together to seal, and knock up with the back of a knife. Brush the top with beaten egg or milk and then bake towards the top of the oven at 220°C/425°F/Gas Mark 7 for 25-30 minutes or until pale gold in colour.

—.—

Wisbech, The Clarkson Memorial 1901 47583

RECIPE

— · —

Apple Dowdy

Juice of half a lemon
300ml/ ½ pint water
675g/1½ lbs cooking apples, peeled, cored and sliced
About 6 slices of stale bread, buttered
Grated nutmeg
50g/2oz golden syrup
25g/1oz soft brown sugar

Pre-heat the oven to 180°C/350°F/Gas Mark 4.

Put the water and lemon juice into a bowl, add the sliced apples and leave for a few minutes. Line a greased pie dish with the buttered bread, buttered sides in, cutting them to fit where necessary, and reserving enough slices to make a 'lid'. Drain the apples and arrange them in the pie dish, sprinkling them with a little grated nutmeg. Gently heat the golden syrup and 1 tablespoonful of water in a small saucepan until the syrup is thin and runny, then pour it over the apples, and sprinkle them with the brown sugar. Cover the apples with a layer of the reserved buttered bread. Cover the pie dish with foil and bake in a pre-heated oven for 45 minutes to 1 hour, until the apples are soft.

— · —

Thape

'Thape' is an old Suffolk word for a gooseberry. Whit Sunday in May was traditionally celebrated in Suffolk with a gooseberry or 'thape' pie, served with custard.

Southwold, The Market 1896 38627

RECIPE

— . —

Greengage Mould

The greengage, or green plum, is named after Sir William Gage, who lived at Hengrave Hall in Suffolk. Cambridgeshire has its own variety of this fruit, known as the Cambridge Gage.

> 350g/12oz greengages
> 75g/3oz soft brown sugar
> 75g/3oz cornflour
> 900ml/1½ pints milk

Place the greengages into a heavy-bottomed saucepan with just enough water to prevent the bottom of the pan from burning. Stew the greengages until they are tender, then remove the stones and pass the fruit pulp through a sieve. Mix the cornflour with a little of the milk to make a smooth paste. Add the sugar to the rest of the milk in a saucepan and bring to the boil, stirring constantly so that the sugar dissolves and does not burn on the bottom of the pan. Pour some of the boiling milk on to the cornflour and mix well, then add the cornflour mixture to the rest of the milk in the pan. Stir the mixture continually whilst it continues to boil until it thickens. Add the greengage pulp and stir the mixture over a low heat for a few more minutes, then remove from heat and leave to stand and cool slightly. Wet the inside of a mould or glass dish, and pour in the mixture. Put into the fridge to set and chill before serving.

— . —

Woodbridge, The River Bank 1898 42772

RECIPE

—·—

Summer Pudding

From the end of the 19th century, the fruit industry around Wisbech in Cambridgeshire started to develop in earnest, and the town and district began to gain a reputation as a centre for the production of high quality fruits, such as strawberries, gooseberries, apples, pears etc. The area of Essex around Tiptree and Elsenham is also famous for its soft fruit and jam-making industry, being particularly known for raspberries and redcurrants. All this soft fruit is ideal for making Summer Pudding.

> 10 slices of crustless white bread – use bread from a proper loaf, not a sliced and
> wrapped one, for best results
> 3 tablespoonfuls of milk
> 750g/1½ lbs soft fruit – use a variety of such fruits as raspberries, cherries,
> redcurrants, blackcurrants, white currants, loganberries or (sparingly) strawberries
> 115g/4oz caster sugar

Reserve a few pieces of fresh fruit to decorate. Lightly butter a pudding basin of 1 litre/1¾ pint capacity. Moisten the bread with milk. Hull, stone or top and tail the fruit as necessary. Cook it all very gently in the sugar for 4-5 minutes until the sugar melts and the juices run. Spoon off a few spoonfuls of the juice as it cools and reserve.

Line the sides and bottom of the pudding basin with the bread slices, cutting them to fit where necessary and checking that there are no spaces. Reserve enough bread slices for a lid. Pour in the fruit, which should come almost to the top, and cover closely with the remaining bread. Put a small plate over the top (it should just fit inside the rim of the basin), and weight it with something heavy. Leave to press overnight in the fridge.

To serve, remove the weight and the plate. Place a deep serving dish over the top of the pudding basin and reverse quickly so that the pudding comes out easily in one piece. Pour the remaining juices slowly all over the pudding, especially over the places where the juice has not seeped through thoroughly. Keep cold.

—·—

Tiptree, Messing Maypole Mill c1955   T116021

TEATIME AND BAKING

Thorpeness, The House in the Clouds and the Mill c1955 T38012

RECIPE

Suffolk Cakes

115g/4oz butter
4 eggs
225g/8oz caster sugar
Grated zest of ½ lemon
115g/4oz self-raising flour

Pre-heat the oven to 200°C/400°F/Gas Mark 6.

Warm the butter so that it is just liquid but not coloured. Separate the eggs and beat the whites until they hold a peak. In a separate bowl, beat the egg yolks and add the sugar and grated lemon zest, then fold this mixture into the beaten egg whites. Mix in the melted butter and stir in the flour. Beat well, and turn into greased bun tins or patty pans. Bake in the pre-heated oven for 10-15

Felixstowe, From the Beach 1899 44513

RECIPE

— · —

Norfolk Vinegar Cake

This is an old Norfolk farmhouse recipe for a good, simple fruit cake. The recipe needs no eggs, and was probably made by the farmer's wife at the times when the hens were not laying.

225g/8oz butter
450g/1 lb plain flour
225g/8oz sugar
225g/8oz raisins
225g/8oz sultanas
250ml/8 fl oz milk
2 tablespoonfuls wine or cider vinegar
1 teaspoonful bicarbonate of soda, mixed with 1 tablespoonful of milk

Pre-heat the oven to 180°C/350°F/Gas Mark 4.

Rub the butter into the flour to give a crumb-like consistency, then mix in the sugar and the fruit. Put the milk into a large jug or bowl and add the vinegar. Pour the bicarbonate of soda and milk mixture into the milk and vinegar – it will froth up and may overflow, so it is wise to hold it over the mixing bowl while doing this.

Stir the liquid into the cake mixture, beat well and put it into a well-greased 23cm (9 inch) cake tin. Bake in the pre-heated oven for 30 minutes, then reduce the heat to 150°C/300°F/Gas Mark 2 and bake for a further 1¼ hours. Cover the top of the cake with foil if it starts to darken.

This cake will keep up to a week in an airtight container, and the flavour improves all the time.

— · —

Garboldisham, Harvest Time c1955 G188029

RECIPE

— · —

Suffolk Fourses Cake

This traditional lardy bread was served to Suffolk harvesters in the afternoons, together with a sweetened beer known as 'sugar beer'. It was probably named 'fourses' because it was served at the four o'clock break, although the name may also relate to the custom of marking the bread into four sections which was followed in some areas of Suffolk.

675g/1½ lbs strong plain flour
1 level teaspoonful salt
2 teaspoonfuls ground mixed spice
175g/6oz lard, softened
15g/ ½ oz dried yeast
2 teaspoonfuls sugar
450ml/ ¾ pint warm water
175g/6oz currants
A little milk to glaze

Mix the yeast with the sugar and a little of the warmed water, and keep in a warm place until it has frothed up.

Sift the flour, salt and spice into a bowl. Rub in the lard and add the creamed yeast mixture. Stir in the remaining water and mix to a smooth, pliable dough. Knead the dough thoroughly, then cover the bowl with a cloth and leave to rise in a warm place until the dough has doubled in size. Knock back, and knead in the currants. Either shape the dough into loaves and put into 450g/1 lb loaf tins, or shape it in to a large round and place on a greased baking sheet, and leave to rise again. If you are making the round loaf version, it is now traditional to mark the top of the loaf into four sections with a sharp knife. Brush the top with milk to glaze, and bake in a hot oven (200°C/400°F/Gas Mark 6) for 45 minutes, until well risen and golden brown.

— · —

King's Lynn, High Street 1908 60024

RECIPE

— · —

Nelson Squares

This recipe recalls one of West Norfolk's most famous sons, Admiral Lord Nelson, who was born at Burnham Thorpe near King's Lynn in 1758. Replace the mixed peel with an extra 50g/2oz of dried fruit, if preferred.

> 225g/8oz stale white bread, with crusts removed
> 300ml/ ½ pint milk
> 115g/4oz currants or raisins, or a mixture of both
> 50g/2oz mixed peel, finely chopped
> 50g/2oz suet
> 50g/2oz demerara sugar
> 1-2 level teaspoonfuls mixed spice, to taste
> 1 egg for the mixture
> 500g/1 lb shortcrust pastry or puff pastry
> 1 beaten egg or a little extra milk for sealing and glazing the pastry

Soak the bread in the milk for half an hour, then beat out any lumps to leave a smooth mixture. Add the dried fruit, mixed peel, suet, sugar and mixed spice and mix well. Mix in the egg, and add a little extra milk if the mixture is too stiff to spread easily.

Pre-heat the oven to 180°C/350°F/Gas Mark 4. Grease a deep 22cm (9 inch) square baking tin. Roll out the pastry and cut into two sections, making one approx 28cm (11 inches) square, and the other approx 22cm (9 inches) square. Use the bigger section to line the base of the baking tin – the pastry should come up the sides of the tin. Spread the fruit mixture evenly over the pastry in the tin, leaving a slight gap around the sides. Brush the edge of the pastry with some of the beaten egg or milk, cover the mixture with the other square of pastry and pinch the edges together with the bottom layer to seal them together and enclose the mixture. Brush the surface with milk or beaten egg and prick some holes in the surface with a fork. Bake in the oven for 1½ to 2 hours, until the pastry is golden brown. Leave to cool in the tin then turn out, sprinkle with sugar and cut into squares before serving.

— · —

Norfolk Dialect Words

'Afront' - in front.

'Ahind' - behind.

'Atwin' - between.

'Bishy barney bee' - a ladybird.

'Dudder' - to shiver.

'Harnser' - a heron.

'Lollop' - to move along slowly.

'Luggy' - deaf.

'Mardle' - to gossip or chat.

'Mavish' - a thrush.

'Mawkin' - a scarecrow.

'Mawther' - a young woman.

'Titty-totty' - very small.

'Uhmtie-tump' - a mole hill.

'Warmint' - vermin, or a varmint, a troublesome person.

RECIPE

—·—

God's Kitchel Cake

It was a particular Suffolk custom for children to visit their godparents at Christmas time and ask for their blessings. A small cake called a God's kitchel was specially made for visiting godchildren. There was an old saying: 'Ask me a blessing and I will give you a kitchel', and in Chaucer's 'Canterbury Tales', written in 1386, we find the lines: 'Give us a bushel, wheat, malt or rye, A God's kitchel, or a trip of cheese.'

> 450g/1 lb made-up flaky pastry
> 115g/4oz margarine
> 225g/8oz currants
> 25g/1oz sultanas
> 50g/2oz candied peel
> 75g/3oz sugar
> 50g/2oz ground almonds
> 1 teaspoonful powdered cinnamon
> 1 teaspoonful grated nutmeg

Melt the margarine in a large saucepan. Add the dried fruit, peel, sugar, ground almonds and spiced. Mix well. Halve the pastry and roll one piece across into a square about 30cm (12 inches) across – it should be rolled quite thin. Place it on a baking sheet. Moisten the edges of the rolled pastry with milk or water, and spread the filling on it, leaving an edge of about 1cm (half an inch). Cover with the second piece of pastry, rolled out to fit. Seal the edges well by pressing lightly together. Carefully mark the top of the cake with a knife into 6cm (2½ inch) squares, but without cutting through the pastry. Bake near the top of a pre-heated oven, 220°C/425°F/Gas Mark 7 until nicely golden brown.

Sprinkle with caster sugar and leave to cool for a few minutes, then divide into sections and leave them to cool on a wire rack.

—·—

Ipswich, Buttermarket 1893 32204

RECIPE

—·—

Saffron Cake

Saffron Walden got its name from the saffron obtained from the stamens of the crocus 'sativus', which was cultivated in great numbers to the north of the town by 'crockers' in 'gardens' in the Middle Ages. Saffron is used as a seasoning and colouring agent in cooking, giving food a golden-yellow colour. For centuries saffron has been the world's most expensive spice, by weight.

> 75g/3oz caster sugar
> 300ml/ ½ pint warm water
> 2 teaspoonfuls of dried yeast
> 450g/1 lb strong plain flour
> 1 teaspoonful salt
> A good pinch of saffron
> 115g/4oz lard
> 115g/4oz currants or raisins
> 75g/3oz butter or margarine
> Beaten egg, to glaze

Dissolve 1 teaspoonful of the caster sugar in the warm water, add the yeast and mix well, then leave in a warm place until it has become frothy.

Sieve the flour, salt and saffron together, then rub in 15g/ ½ oz of the lard. Gradually add in the yeast mixture, and work it all together to make a firm dough. Knead the dough on a floured surface for 10 minutes or so until it has become smooth and elastic. Put the dough in bowl covered with a damp cloth and leave to 'prove' in a warm place until it has doubled in size. When the dough has risen, melt the remaining lard and the butter or margarine together. Work the melted fats, the remaining sugar and the dried fruit into the dough, and knead it all for a further 10 minutes. Leave the dough in a covered bowl in a warm place for a further 30 minutes, until it has risen again.

Pre-heat the oven to 190°C/375°F/Gas Mark 5.

Turn the dough into a well-greased 1kg/2 lb loaf tin, and brush the top of the cake with beaten egg. Bake in the pre-heated oven for 40-45 minutes, or until it is risen and cooked through – cover the top with foil if it starts to brown too much. Leave in the tin for about 15 minutes before turning out on to a wire tray to cool. Store in an airtight container and serve sliced, spread with butter.

—·—

Saffron Walden, High Street 1919 69134

RECIPE

—·—

Suffolk Apple Cake

225g/8oz plain flour
1½ tablespoonfuls baking powder
A pinch of salt
115g/4oz lard
50g/2oz caster sugar
225g/8oz cooking apples
A little milk

Pre-heat the oven to 190°C/375°F/Gas Mark 5.

Grease a baking sheet. Sift the flour, baking powder and salt into a mixing basin. Rub in the dripping or lard until the mixture resembles breadcrumbs, and stir in the sugar. Peel and core the apples and chop them into small pieces, or grate them. Add the apples to the other ingredients, together with enough milk to make a firm dough. Form the dough into a round, flat cake about 0.5cm (quarter inch) thick. Place the dough on the greased baking sheet and bake in the pre-heated oven for about 45 minutes, until the cake is well-risen and golden. Eat the cake hot, cut into wedges, split open and spread with butter.

—·—

Honey for Tea?

The last two lines of Rupert Brooke's poem, 'The Old Vicarage, Grantchester', have immortalised the church of this village a few miles from Cambridge:

'Stands the church clock at ten to three
And is there honey still for tea?

It is believed that the church clock was actually broken and stuck at ten to three when the poet was living in Grantchester. For years after Brooke's death in the First World War, the clock was kept at ten to three as a memorial to him. The nearby Grantchester Tea Rooms houses an excellent collection of photographs and exhibits about the poet and his contemporaries.

Grantchester, The Church of St Andrew and St Mary
1929 81771

MISCELLANEOUS

—·—

RECIPE

—·—

Norfolk Rusks

175g/6oz self-raising flour
A good pinch of salt
70g/2½ oz margarine
1 beaten egg

Pre-heat the oven to 200°C/400°F/Gas Mark 6.

Sift the flour and salt into a bowl, and rub in the margarine. Mix to a firm dough with the egg. Roll out on a floured board to 7mm (¼ inch) thick, cut into rounds and place on a baking sheet. Bake in the pre-heated oven, for 15-20 minutes until golden. Remove from oven and, when cool enough to handle, split each rusk in half with a sharp knife. Return the rusks to the oven, cut side up, for 5 minutes longer to dry and colour a little, then turn on to a cooling wire. Keep in an airtight tin. These are delicious spread with butter, and served with cheese.

—·—

Overstrand, The Sands 1906 56868

RECIPE

Cambridge Sauce

This makes a piquant, savoury sauce.

> 6 hard-boiled eggs
> 300m/½ pint olive oil
> 4 anchovy fillets
> 2 tablespoonfuls mixed finely chopped chervil, tarragon, and chives
> 1 tablespoonful mustard
> 1 tablespoonful vinegar
> 1 teaspoonful capers
> 1 teaspoonful finely chopped parsley
> Cayenne pepper to taste

Blend the eggs, anchovy fillets, capers and mixed herbs together into a smooth paste, using a food processor or pestle and mortar. Slowly whisk in the oil and vinegar, and season with pepper. Stir in the chopped parsley before serving.

St Ives, Bridge Street 1898 41280

85

RECIPE

~ . ~

Yarmouth Biscuits

350g/12oz plain flour
175g/6oz currants
225g/8oz butter
225g/8oz caster sugar
3 eggs, beaten

Pre-heat the oven to 190°C/375°F/Gas Mark 5.

Grease two baking sheets. Mix together the currants, butter, sugar, flour and beaten eggs to make a thick paste. Roll out on a floured surface and cut into rounds. Place on the greased baking sheets and bake for 15-20 minutes, until the biscuits are golden brown.

~ . ~

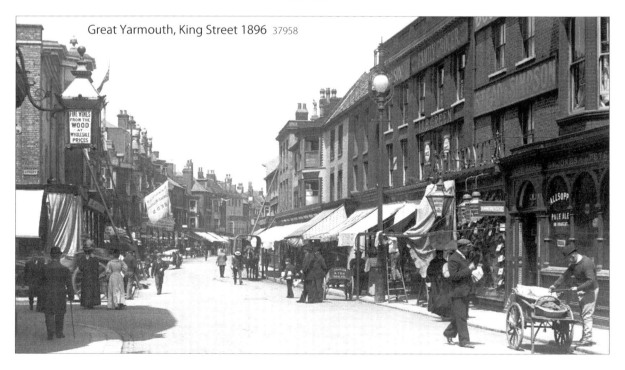

Great Yarmouth, King Street 1896 37958

INDEX OF PHOTOGRAPHS

INDEX OF RECIPES

FRITH PRODUCTS & SERVICES

Francis Frith would doubtless be pleased to know that the pioneering publishing venture he started in 1860 still continues today. Over a hundred and forty years later, The Francis Frith Collection continues in the same innovative tradition and is now one of the foremost publishers of vintage photographs in the world. Some of the current activities include:

INTERIOR DECORATION

Today Frith's photographs can be seen framed and as giant wall murals in thousands of pubs, restaurants, hotels, banks, retail stores and other public buildings throughout the country. In every case they enhance the unique local atmosphere of the places they depict and provide reminders of gentler days in an increasingly busy and frenetic world.

PRODUCT PROMOTIONS

Frith products are used by many major companies to promote the sales of their own products or to reinforce their own history and heritage. Frith promotions have been used by Hovis bread, Courage beers, Scots Porage Oats, Colman's mustard, Cadbury's foods, Mellow Birds coffee, Dunhill pipe tobacco, Guinness, and Bulmer's Cider.

GENEALOGY AND FAMILY HISTORY

As the interest in family history and roots grows world-wide, more and more people are turning to Frith's photographs of Great Britain for images of the towns, villages and streets where their ancestors lived; and, of course, photographs of the churches and chapels where their ancestors were christened, married and buried are an essential part of every genealogy tree and family album.

FRITH PRODUCTS

All Frith photographs are available Framed or just as Mounted Prints and Posters (size 23 x 16 inches). These may be ordered from the address below. Other products available are- Address Books, Calendars, Jigsaws, Canvas Prints, Notelets and local and prestige books.

THE INTERNET

Already ninety thousand Frith photographs can be viewed and purchased on the internet through the Frith websites and a myriad of partner sites.

For more detailed information on Frith companies and products, look at this site:
www.francisfrith.com

See the complete list of Frith Books at: www.francisfrith.com
This web site is regularly updated with the latest list of publications from The Francis Frith Collection. If you wish to buy books relating to another part of the country that your local bookshop does not stock, you may purchase on-line.

For further information, trade, or author enquiries please contact us at the address below:
The Francis Frith Collection, Unit 6, Oakley Business Park, Wylye Road, Dinton, Wiltshire SP3 5EU.
Tel: +44 (0)1722 716 376 Fax: +44 (0)1722 716 881 Email: sales@francisfrith.co.uk

---

See Frith products on the internet at www.francisfrith.com

FREE PRINT OF YOUR CHOICE

Mounted Print
Overall size 14 x 11 inches (355 x 280mm)

Choose any Frith photograph in this book.
Simply complete the Voucher opposite and return it with your remittance for £3.50 (to cover postage and handling) and we will print the photograph of your choice in SEPIA (size 11 x 8 inches) and supply it in a cream mount with a burgundy rule line (overall size 14 x 11 inches).
Please note: aerial photographs and photographs with a reference number starting with a "Z" are not Frith photographs and cannot be supplied under this offer. Offer valid for delivery to one UK address only.

PLUS: **Order additional Mounted Prints at HALF PRICE - £9.50 each** (normally £19.00)
If you would like to order more Frith prints from this book, possibly as gifts for friends and family, you can buy them at half price (with no additional postage and handling costs).

PLUS: **Have your Mounted Prints framed**
For an extra £18.00 per print you can have your mounted print(s) framed in an elegant polished wood and gilt moulding, overall size 16 x 13 inches (no additional postage and handling required).

IMPORTANT!

These special prices are only available if you use this form to order. You must use the ORIGINAL VOUCHER on this page (no copies permitted). We can only despatch to one UK address. This offer cannot be combined with any other offer.

Send completed Voucher form to:
The Francis Frith Collection, Unit 6, Oakley Business Park, Wylye Road, Dinton, Wiltshire SP3 5EU

CHOOSE A PHOTOGRAPH FROM THIS BOOK

Voucher for **FREE** and Reduced Price Frith Prints

Please do not photocopy this voucher. Only the original is valid, so please fill it in, cut it out and return it to us with your order.

Picture ref no	Page no	Qty	Mounted @ £9.50	Framed + £18.00	Total Cost £
		1	Free of charge*	£	£
			£9.50	£	£
			£9.50	£	£
			£9.50	£	£
			£9.50	£	£
			£9.50	£	£
Please allow 28 days for delivery. Offer available to one UK address only			* Post & handling		£3.50
			Total Order Cost		£

Title of this book . . . .

I enclose a cheque/postal order for £ . . . .
made payable to 'The Francis Frith Collection'

OR please debit my Mastercard / Visa / Maestro card, details below

Card Number:

Issue No (Maestro only):   Valid from (Maestro):

Card Security Number: Expires:

Signature:

Name Mr/Mrs/Ms . . . .
Address . . . .
. . . .
. . . .
. . . . Postcode . . . .
Daytime Tel No . . . .
Email . . . .

Valid to 31/12/12

Can you help us with information about any of the Frith photographs in this book?

We are gradually compiling an historical record for each of the photographs in the Frith archive. It is always fascinating to find out the names of the people shown in the pictures, as well as insights into the shops, buildings and other features depicted.

If you recognize anyone in the photographs in this book, or if you have information not already included in the author's caption, do let us know. We would love to hear from you, and will try to publish it in future books or articles.

An Invitation from The Francis Frith Collection to Share Your Memories

The 'Share Your Memories' feature of our website allows members of the public to add personal memories relating to the places featured in our photographs, or comment on others already added. Seeing a place from your past can rekindle forgotten or long held memories. Why not visit the website, find photographs of places you know well and add YOUR story for others to read and enjoy? We would love to hear from you!

www.francisfrith.com/memories

Our production team

Frith books are produced by a small dedicated team at offices near Salisbury. Most have worked with the Frith Collection for many years. All have in common one quality: they have a passion for the Frith Collection.

Frith Books and Gifts

We have a wide range of books and gifts available on our website utilising our photographic archive, many of which can be individually personalised.

www.francisfrith.com

Free Print – see overleaf